Planeta Publishers. Moscow, 1989

ISBN 5-85250-161-1

MOSCOW

Written and compiled by
YURI BALANENKO

Photographs by
NIKOLAI RAKHMANOV

Design by
DMITRY BISTI

Translation by
ALEX MILLER

Moscow, the capital of the Union of Soviet Socialist Republics and the Russian Federation, is the political, industrial, historical and cultural centre of the first socialist state in the world.

Highly sophisticated machines and precision instruments are manufactured in Moscow. It was in Moscow that the first routes into space were mapped out. Moscow is as famous for its science institutes, educational establishments, theatres and museums as for its literature, visual arts, music and sports. No capital in the world has known construction projects on such a gigantic scale as Moscow. Supporting the programme of accelerating the development of the whole country, advanced by the 27th Congress of the Communist Party of the Soviet Union, Moscow city residents have set before themselves large-scale tasks and have proceeded to implement them.

Moscow is a hero-city. It honours the memory of victories over many invaders, from the khans of the Golden Horde to Hitler's fascists.

Humanity looks to Moscow for the fulfilment of its hopes and aspirations for a just and stable peace. In his Political Report to the 27th CPSU Congress the General Secretary of the CPSU Central Committee Mikhail Gorbachev said, "Our ideal is a world without weapons and violence, a world in which each people freely chooses its path of development, its way of life. This is an expression of the humanism of Communist ideology, of its moral values. That is why for the future as well **the struggle against the nuclear threat, against the arms race, for the preservation and strengthening of universal peace** remains the fundamental direction of the Party's activities in the international arena."

* * *

One of the world's biggest cities, Moscow is situated in the centre of the East-European Plain approximately on the same latitude as Copenhagen, Edinburgh and Glasgow. Its eight million inhabitants represent over a hundred nationalities.

Covering an area of over eight hundred and seventy square kilometres, Moscow is bigger than New York with its population of sixteen million, two and a half times as big as London and eight times bigger than Paris.

The city extends for 30 kilometres from West to East and for 40 kilometres from North to South. Its planning is quite distinctive: the Moscow avenues radiate outwards like the spokes of a wheel and are linked by a series of concentric rings.

The first ring is formed by the walls of the ancient Kremlin. The main Moscow squares and the remains of the Kitai-Gorod* fortifications are arrayed round them like a necklace. The next ring, in a bend of the Moskva River, is formed by the boulevards. The fortress wall fringing Bely Gorod** followed this ring in the Middle Ages. The names of the squares—Yauzskiye Gates, Pokrovskiye Gates, Petrovskiye Gates and Nikitskiye Gates—testify to ancient times when there really were gates flanked by watch towers in the city walls. The suburbs and fringe settlements of Bely Gorod were ringed with a moat and an earth rampart where the wide Garden Ring (Sadovoye Koltso) now runs.

Ancient times are recalled by the names—Crimean Rampart (Krymsky Val), Earth Rampart (Zemlyanoi Val), Rampart Street (Valovaya Ulitsa)... Roads branched out in all directions from the Kremlin to Tver, Novgorod, Smolensk, Kaluga, Serpukhov... Next comes the steel ring of the Circle Railway, the city's boundary in 1917, linking up the many railway lines running from the capital. The giant ring-radial pattern is completed by the ring of the Moscow Motorway.

The architectural ensembles in these zones—consisting mainly of buildings twelve to sixteen sto-

---

* Kitai-Town (from *kita* — the wattle used in the foundations of the earth rampart round the original fortress).
** White Town. The fortifications were built of limestone.

reys high, with squares, big stores, theatres, hotels and stadiums—vary in colour combinations and layout, but they are all in a natural setting. Moscow's huge parks are virtually inseparable from the region's forests.

The centre of Moscow has taken shape over the centuries inside the Garden Ring, with the Kremlin as its architectural focus. Certain streets and even districts here have become protected zones, and new construction projects are being carried out parallel with the restoration of the ancient monuments. Trunk roads, boulevards, parks and waterways link the city centre with the peripheral zones, giving the Soviet capital its own distinctive appearance.

The Moscow Kremlin is one of the most beautiful architectural ensembles in the world. Its style is a national classic of ancient Russian art and dates back to the traditions of Moscow, Novgorod-Pskov and Vladimir-Suzdal architecture with its austere forms, its colour schemes and its monumentality.

The first reference to Moscow in the chronicles goes back to 1147. Moscow's annals are reckoned from this date, although its primitive history goes back thousands of years. According to the chronicles, in 1156, the Suzdal Prince Yuri Dolgoruky, son of Vladimir Monomakh, had wooden fortifications surrounded by a moat built on Borovitsky Hill at the confluence of the Moskva River, which gave its name to the city, and the Neglinnaya River.

On the intersection not only of land, but of river trade routes, the city gradually acquired great strategic importance over the years.

At the beginning of 1238, Moscow bore the brunt of Khan Batu's hordes as they swarmed westwards. For many long years the land of Russia went to rack and ruin.

In the 14th century, Moscow became a centre for the unification of the Russian principalities for the national-liberation struggle. The foundations of Moscow's might were laid by the shrewd and far-seeing policy of Ivan Kalita. After the fires that destroyed the old Kremlin, Ivan Kalita built a new Kremlin of oak beams in 1339-1340. Its grounds were considerably enlarged. The prince's palace was built on a high hill. In the centre of the square, framed by the stone Cathedral of the Assumption and the Cathedral of the Archangel, stood the Church of St. John Climacus and its bell-tower. The Cathedral of the Archangel subsequently became the burial place of the Moscow princes.

The further growth of Moscow's influence was due to Kalita's grandson, Prince Dmitry Ivanovich. In 1367 he fortified the Kremlin with walls and towers of white stone. This new Kremlin was almost as big as the present one.

Over 600 years ago, in 1380, on Kulikovo Field by the upper reaches of the Don River, warriors representing most of the Russian principalities led by Dmitry defeated the hosts of Mamai, ruler of the Golden Horde. To Russia, this engagement, known to history as the Battle of Kulikovo, was the beginning of the end to the foreign yoke and brought fame to the power of the Russian armies and to the name of the Moscow prince, who from that time on was known as Dmitry Donskoi (of the Don).

After the overthrow of the Golden Horde domination and the unification of the Russian principalities, Moscow became the capital of the centralized state, inaugurating an era of renaissance in the arts. The Kremlin cathedrals were decorated by Theophanes the Greek and Andrei Rublev. In the city's monasteries, books were decorated with miniatures and head-pieces; the wooden covers were bound in leather.

Trading contacts developed with West and East. At the end of the 15th century envoys came to Moscow from Italy, Germany, Livonia, Poland and Hungary. Russian merchants and ambassadors visited the Crimea, Persia, Turkey and even India. Muscovites took part in mastering the sea route round Scandinavia.

Secular literature spread; history, philosophy and

the natural sciences, began to develop further. The new rise of Moscow painting was associated with Dionysius and his school. The finest craftsmen came to Moscow from Pskov, Rostov Veliky and Vladimir. Majestic churches rose up in place of the Kremlin's ramshackle buildings. Later, Italian architects took part in the work, but none of the subsequent structures violated the artistic integrity, harmony and unity of the Kremlin. They merely introduced new touches and deepened the originality of style which formed at that time in Russia. In 1475, Aristotele Fioravanti began building a new Cathedral of the Assumption. The work took four years. Situated in the centre of the Kremlin, the five-domed church impressed the people of that time with its majesty and the harmoniousness of its architectural forms.

The whitestone prince's Cathedral of the Annunciation had been built in 1397; rebuilding began under Ivan the Third. The Pskov craftsmen used the old limestone foundations in 1484-1489 for a new three-domed church of brick. In the 16th century the cathedral was finished and the domes were gilded all over. The Kremlin walls, with their crenellated battlements and towers, were first built under Ivan the Third; they are with us to this day. The work lasted from 1485 to 1495. The new walls, over which rose eighteen towers, were over two kilometres in length, and their thickness varied between 3.5 and 6.5 metres. On the Red Square side a deep moat was dug which, by joining the Neglinnaya River to the Moskva River, converted the Kremlin into an island fortress. Two more towers, the Kutafya and the Tsar's, were built much later.

In the 16th century, Moscow became one of the largest cities in Europe. Foreigners who visited the capital have testified that it was bigger than London, Prague or Florence. The architects of that time left us such magnificent monuments as the Bell-Tower of Ivan the Great, the Cathedral of St. Basil the Blessed and the Kremlin's Cathedral of the Archangel. The formation of a centralized Moscow state was ac-companied by the growth of Russian national literature, the appearance in 1563 of Ivan Fyodorov's printing press, and the development of the book trade and the applied arts.

By that time, Moscow had a population of over 100,000. Most of them were labourers or artisans. The armourers, smiths, jewellers, cannon and bell founders were famous for their skill, and their products for perfection of finish. To this day the names of certain streets, alleys, squares and embankments in Moscow reflect the crafts practised by the population in those times: Cannon Street (Pushechnaya Ulitsa), Cauldron Embankment (Kotelnicheskaya Naberezhnaya), Pottery Embankment (Goncharnaya Naberezhnaya), Musket By-street (Ruzheiny Pereulok).

This period saw the first moves against feudal oppression. In June 1547 the discontent of the people in the *posad* (trading quarter outside the city wall) grew into an open uprising—"the great disturbance". A powerful blow against the serf-owning regime was struck by the peasant war, which lasted from June 1606 to October 1607 under the leadership of Ivan Bolotnikov.

Time passed, and the centralized power gained strength. The tsar's edicts were proclaimed from the Lobnoye Mesto. One day in June 1671, Stepan Razin, the people's hero, was quartered nearby. Before a vast crowd of Muscovites in January 1775, Yemelyan Pugachyov, the hero of the great peasant war, was executed on Bolotnaya Square. Both before and after these events, Moscow was shaken by the ominous rumblings of popular discontent. So it was during the city uprisings of 1648 and 1662, and during the mutinies of the *streltsy* (originally the tsar's bodyguard) in 1682 and 1698.

The second half of the 17th century in Moscow saw successes in education and the intensified spread of literacy among the population. There was an increasing demand for translated literature, and books in Russian and the Slavonic languages appeared on sale. In the Zaikonospassky Monastery on Nikolskaya Street, the Slavic-Graeco-Latin Academy, the first higher educational establishment in Russia, was founded with the prominent public figure, scholar and poet, Simeon Polotsky, as its director. To Mikhail Lomonosov, a graduate from that academy, a man of the people, scholar and self-taught genius, the city owes the subsequent foundation of Moscow University, which was to play a vital part in Russian science and culture.

Dmitry Ukhtomsky was an outstanding Moscow architect in the mid-18th century. Builder of the five-tiered bell-tower in the Trinity-Sergius Monastery, the Church of St. Nicetas the Martyr and many other buildings, Ukhtomsky was also famous as a gifted teacher. His pupils included such remarkable master craftsmen as Vasily Bazhenov and Matvei Kazakov.

From a design by Bazhenov in 1784-1786, a magnificent house was built on the crest of a small hill at the beginning of Mokhovaya Street (now Marx Avenue). First known as "Pashkov's House", it later became the Rumyantsev Museum. It is now the old building of the Lenin State Library of the USSR.

Sixty buildings were put up in Moscow from designs by Kazakov, including the present House of Unions, the Municipal Hospital on Petrovka Street, the Moscow City Soviet, and Moscow University, built in 1786-1793. Russian classical architecture is at its most impressive in the Petrovsky Palace, also built from a design by Kazakov. The high stone wall with its corner towers is reminiscent of an ancient fortress.

Under Peter the Great in 1712 the capital was transferred to St. Petersburg, the new city on the Neva. Moscow, however, continued to be the centre of Russia's cultural life and the vehicle for the expression of the nation's patriotism, which manifested itself with particular power during the struggle against the Napoleonic invasion.

The 19th century began dramatically: Napoleon's armies trampled all over Western Europe. In 1812 Napoleonic hordes burst into Russia. Silent but grim memorials of those days stand on the Field of Borodino outside Moscow. Almost a hundred and thirty years later, the Field of Borodino was to become the scene of another bloody battle, this time with the German fascist invaders.

The past comes to life again in the History Museum and in the Borodino Museum outside Moscow, as well as in the halls of the circular building of the Battle of Borodino Panorama. The famous Triumphal Arch in honour of the victory over Napoleon has been restored on Kutuzovsky Avenue.

The entry of the French into Moscow was accompanied by a great fire. Fortunately, the Kremlin survived, but there was some damage to the bellcote, the Extension of the Metropolitan Filaret, the Ivan the Great Bell-Tower, several of the wall towers, and the Arsenal. The city suffered seriously, with two-thirds of the houses destroyed by fire.

Soon after the defeat of Napoleon, a special "commission for buildings in Moscow" was set up under Bove, one of Kazakov's pupils. This architect took part in the designing and building of the Bolshoi Theatre and the layout of the adjacent square; he also directed work on the Alexandrovsky Gardens and helped with the architectural finishing touches to the Manège.

Moscow rose again from the ashes and was enriched by new architectural ensembles. The city's industry also recovered rapidly. Russian industrial goods appeared for the first time at the Leipzig Fair in 1828.

After the Crimean War of 1853-1856 the revolutionary situation in the land came to a crisis. Drawing inspiration from Utopian socialism, the *Raznochintsy* (revolutionary intellectuals not of gentle birth) attempted to struggle for the country's liberation from the leftovers of the serf system. The ideology of the *Narodnik* (populist) movement took shape. Proletarian circles, however, still lacked a wide movement and a solid organization. The rising tide of revolution was suppressed by the autocracy.

The architecture in the second half of the 19th and the beginning of the 20th century reflected the predominance of bourgeois taste. The houses built were largely intended for profit, and next to the private houses of the factory owners stood the much smaller ones of the officials and the tiny hovels of the artisans, while the working-class districts on the outskirts of the city were mainly barracks.

Marxism began to spread through Russia at the end of the 19th century, and Lenin took the path of revolutionary struggle. The Social-Democratic Workers' Union was formed in Moscow on Lenin's initiative, and the first Moscow Committee of the Russian Social-Democratic Labour Party was founded in 1898.

After the shooting down of workers in St. Petersburg in January 1905, the country was swept by a wave of strikes and peasant demonstrations: in June the red flag of the revolution was hoisted by the Battleship *Potyomkin*; in September the workers of Moscow began a political strike. Events were leading irrevocably to the December armed uprising of the Moscow proletariat.

Those days have gone down in the history of Moscow and are forever alive in the memory of the people. They are recorded in the names of streets, squares, embankments, gardens and parks. Uprising Square (Ploshchad Vosstaniya) is one of the examples. Here, in bitter fighting with the tsar's troops the revolutionaries fought to the death while covering the approaches to the working-class quarters of the Presnya. Barricade Street (Barrikadnaya Ulitsa) can also testify to the revolutionary past: during the first Russian revolution, here, as in many other places, the fighting detachments built defences with chopped down telegraph poles, old roofs, doors wrenched off their hinges, notice boards and window frames.

The first Russian revolution had a powerful impact on the international working-class and national-liberation movement. Lenin emphasized: "Without such a dress rehearsal as we had in 1905, the revolution of 1917—both the bourgeois, February revolution, and the proletarian, October revolution— would have been impossible."

Four months later, on 11 March 1918, after the victory of the Great October Socialist Revolution, the Soviet government, headed by Lenin, moved from Petrograd to Moscow. The great founder of the Communist Party and the Soviet state now lived and worked in the Kremlin.

On 10 July 1918, the Fifth All-Russia Congress of Soviets adopted the first Constitution of the RSFSR, in which Moscow was declared the capital of the country, the unifying centre of the free peoples in the Russian Federation.

On 30 December 1922 the First All-Union Congress of Soviets was held in the Bolshoi Theatre in Moscow. It passed the Declaration on the Formation of the USSR, in which was written the following: "Moscow is the capital of the Union of Soviet Socialist Republics."

Moscow assumed her new historical role under unusual, complex and difficult circumstances. The imperialist war, devastation and famine made life hard to bear for the overwhelming majority of workers. But in spite of these difficulties, the features of a socialist city were clearly beginning to emerge.

The Moscow Soviet began its activities by rehousing the poor in the bourgeois quarters. The Soviet authorities confiscated the clubs of the bourgeois landowner upper class, converting them into workers' palaces where lectures were given and concerts were staged for the working people. In 1919, the first *Rabfak* (workers' school) made its appearance; its function was to prepare the workers for study at higher schools.

Scientific projects and programmes of far-reaching scope were under way in the young Soviet capital. Lenin's plan for the electrification of Russia (GOELRO) envisaged the solution of many technical, scientific, economic and social problems, raising the backward country to the level of world civilization in general. This plan was, in effect, the beginning of a vast scientific and technical revolution that was to take Soviet Moscow to the forefront of scientific and technical progress in the 20th century.

During the difficult years of the Civil War and the foreign intervention, when all forces were mobilized to defend the gains of October, Lenin was already thinking of replanning the capital. The leader of the revolution dreamed of the time when Moscow would become a beautiful socialist city.

On Lenin's initiative architects began drawing up plans for improvements. Lenin stressed that during reconstruction it was essential to preserve the ancient architectural monuments, everything of value that had been created by the artistic genius of the Russian people. In October 1918 a nation-wide inventory of the country's historical and artistic treasures was begun. Reconstruction and restoration work was carried out in the Kremlin and on Red Square.

In the second half of the 1920s, the Soviet Union experienced a spectacular industrial and cultural upsurge. New factories, scientific research centres, educational establishments, theatres, museums and stadiums were built in the capital. The population was rapidly increasing.

The 1935 General Plan for the Reconstruction of Moscow became the first document in history to determine the basic principles of socialist town planning. This plan was improved and augmented in subsequent years and Moscow began to undergo a major transformation thanks to extensive work on the reconstruction of the main roads and squares and to the improvement of the entire municipal administration.

A broad thoroughfare, now Marx Avenue, replaced what had once been the Okhotny Ryad (Game Market). The House of the USSR Council of Ministers (now the State Planning Committee of the USSR) and the *Moskva* Hotel went up here. Gorky Street acquired a new look. It was straightened and

made two and a half times as wide to become a beautiful contemporary thoroughfare. The most valuable buildings were moved back from the roadway, and two storeys were added to the Moscow City Soviet building after it had been transferred to the inner part of the quarter.

Improvements were made to Dzerzhinsky, Revolution, Sverdlov, Kommuna, Sovietskaya, Novaya, Staraya and Smolenskaya squares, and also to Marx Avenue. Manezhnaya Square formed in this way (now Pyatidesyatiletiye Oktyabrya Square) gave a view of the Alexandrovsky Gardens, Marx Avenue, Herzen and Gorky streets, Revolution Square and the Manège—the latter a magnificent monument of Russian classical architecture dating back to the beginning of the 19th century.

Unique new buildings appeared: the Lenin State Library of the USSR, the Central Theatre of the Soviet Army, the Frunze Academy, the *Dynamo* Stadium, the Tchaikovsky Concert Hall, Khimki River Station, and many others.

But this vigorous and determined reconstruction was delayed for a long time by the war that fascist Germany imposed on the Soviet Union.

The restoration of the municipal economy and then the building of living accommodation and cultural facilities on a vast scale by industrial methods began in the years of the first post-war five-year plan. In 1951 the Soviet government confirmed a ten-year plan for the reconstruction of the city, while retaining the main features of the first General Plan. A powerful industrial base was built up in record time. New housing estates began to go up on the Peschaniye streets and in Cheryomushki, Kuzminki and Izmailovo. Linking the profile of the city with the outlines of the Kremlin towers, high-rise residential and office blocks went up on Smolenskaya, Vosstaniye and Lermontovskaya squares and Kotelnicheskaya Embankment. The *Ukraina* Hotel was built on Kutuzovsky Avenue, the *Leningradskaya* Hotel on Komsomolskaya Square, and Moscow State University on Lenin Hills.

One after another came the Council for Mutual Economic Assistance, the Young Pioneer Palace on Lenin Hills, the All-Union Television Centre at Ostankino, the *Rossiya* Hotel, the Central Air Terminal and the *Moskva* General Stores. A gigantic architectural ensemble appeared on Kalinin Prospekt. New bridges were built, flyovers, tunnels, and countless pedestrian subways.

The National Economic Achievements Exhibition has become a kind of "country within a city". The three hundred hectares of park land are dotted with palatial pavilions in which the visitors can see everything new being produced in the Soviet Union and what is being done by the scientists, engineers and agricultural workers of all the 15 constituent Soviet Union republics. In particular, the visitor can study a replica of the rocket which on April 12, 1961 carried Yuri Gagarin into space.

The accomplishment of this immense building programme has radically changed the appearance of the city.

Even more beautiful now, the Kremlin is the permanent residence of the highest legislative and executive bodies of state power, the Supreme Soviet of the USSR, and the Council of Ministers of the USSR. All the Kremlin buildings, historical, artistic and architectural monuments are protected and meticulously maintained and restored by the state. Five ancient Kremlin towers—the Trinity, the St. Nicholas, the Saviour, the Water and the Borovitskaya—have been surmounted with shining five-pointed stars symbolizing the new Moscow.

The Kremlin Palace of Congresses, a fine example of contemporary monumental architecture, built in 1961, is known all over the world as the venue for CPSU congresses. They formulate domestic and foreign policies of the Communist Party and Soviet government, plans of Communist construction, and programmes designed to ensure world peace.

The Lenin Mausoleum in Red Square is regarded with great reverence by the Soviet people. From inside the Alexandrovsky Gardens, adjacent to the Kremlin, a seemingly endless queue winds its way past the Eternal Flame on the Grave of the Unknown Soldier and across the square to the Mausoleum.

In June 1971 a new General Plan for the Development of Moscow was confirmed.

Moscow is building, developing, improving without end. In the last years many vast housing estates have grown up, each situated in beautiful natural surroundings and accommodating 250,000-300,000 people. The Central Concert Hall in the *Rossiya* Hotel, the new State Circus on Vernadsky Avenue, the new theatre on Tverskoi Boulevard, the Central House of Artists near Krymsky Bridge, the *Cosmos* Hotel—all went up at about the same time.

Preparations for the Games of the 22nd Olympiad became an integral part of the programme for improving the conditions of work, life and leisure for Muscovites.

One of the major international sports centres, the Soviet capital boasted many facilities well up to the rigorous Olympic standards even before the preparations for the Olympics. In spite of this, 78 projects were incorporated into the Olympic building programme, including 12 unique new structures. Some of them are highly contemporary in architecture, engineering techniques and dimensions.

The main sports arena, the reconstructed Lenin Stadium, accommodates 103,000 spectators. The open-air swimming pool and the Small Sports Arena have been modernized at Luzhniki, and the *Druzhba* Multi-Purpose Sports Hall, like a giant tortoise in shape, has become the pride of the complex. After the Olympics, these sports centres are used for all-Union and international contests and, once every four years, for the finals of the Summer Spartakiad of the Peoples of the USSR, in which foreign athletes also take part.

In 1986 Moscow hosted the Goodwill Games, a large international festival with the participation of sportsmen from five continents.

Extensive work is under way to reconstruct the city and restore the old monuments that are cherished by the people and especially by native Muscovites. That is why city builders are now facing an extremely difficult task of how to strike a balance between the old and the new, how to keep intact the precious monumental heritage of the past against the background of a modern cityscape. The state keeps this problem in sight at all times.

By the mid-90s, according to the programme for the social and economic development of Moscow, it is planned to build sixteen million square metres of living-space, providing each family with a separate flat by the year 2000.

Moscow transport is being developed further. The first line of the Moscow Metro began running back in 1935. The construction of this convenient form of city transport is continuing further. In 1983 another line went into operation, Serpukhovskaya, which links the Circle Line with the southern outskirts of Moscow. The Metro now has 138 stations and over 220 kilometres of underground track.

Muscovites also use waterways for pleasure trips and visits to the rest zones. Some 25 city and suburban lines operate on the Moskva River. They are serviced by motor ships and hydrofoils. You can sail from Moscow to Astrakhan or Leningrad in a comfortable ship. The Moskva Canal links the capital with five seas—the White, the Baltic, the Caspian, the Black Sea and the Sea of Azov. This waterway runs through a system of locks linking Khimki Reservoir with the Moskva River, which lies 30 metres below.

Over a million passengers are catered for every 24 hours by the capital's nine railway termini, and over 15,000,000 people pass every year through the airports of Vnukovo, Domodedovo, Sheremetyevo and Bykovo. Moscow's airfields welcome planes from some 30 foreign companies. In its turn Aeroflot's liners regularly visit the airports of 98 other countries.

Millions of tourists visit Moscow annually and familiarize themselves with the finest examples of Soviet multinational art, with the masterpieces in the Tretyakov Gallery now being renovated and the Pushkin Fine Arts Museum, with the cultural monuments in and around Moscow, and with the sights of the Moscow Kremlin.

The Moscow Kremlin is a great witness of world history. Its beauty is sung by poets and composers, and it has been the subject of books by writers and scholars. It never fails to impress anyone who has seen it even if only once, or who has heard the Kremlin carillons. In the Kremlin the history of Russia comes to life, recalling the names of superb Russian master craftsmen, artists and architects. No one will ever forget the thrill of seeing the treasures in the Armoury, the Diamond Collection, the work of Theophanes the Greek, Andrei Rublev, Dionysius, the Matorins, father and son (the skilled foundrymen who cast the Tsar-Bell 250 years ago) or Andrei Chokhov, who made the Tsar-Cannon.

Spring and autumn, winter and summer, the early glow of dawn and the sinking fire of the sunset, the sudden summer rain and the light whisper of the Russian snowfall are equally beautiful and unforgettable in Moscow. On a clear day, seen from Lenin Hills, the vast city lies spread out before your eyes so that you can trace the bends in the streets or the wide valleys of the squares; and when the city lights cast their warm glow up into the night sky, the Kremlin seems to be sailing in mid-air over Moscow.

Muscovites are hospitable and warm-hearted. They love their city and are proud of it. They will do everything possible to make it more beautiful and comfortable. "Welcome!" they say to all who wish to visit Moscow and be the guests of the Soviet capital.

Every newcomer to the Soviet capital
first goes to see Red Square.

The Lenin Mausoleum stands at the centre of Red Square. There is always a guard of honour at the entrance. The ceremony of the changing of the guard commences at the exact moment when the musical chimes of the Kremlin clock announce the beginning of another hour in the life of the land.

On revolutionary holidays, Red Square becomes the scene of festive processions by working people and of military parades.

In November 1987, all progressive people celebrated the 70th anniversary of the Great October Socialist Revolution. This festive day is closely associated with the name of Vladimir Ilyich Lenin, a titan of scientific thought, a fiery revolutionary, the founder and leader of the Communist Party and the world's first socialist state. Lenin dedicated the whole of his life to the struggle for the social liberation of the proletariat and all the oppressed masses, and for the happiness of the working people.

Following Lenin's behests, the Land of Soviets has become a mighty industrial power with vast economic and techno-logical potentialities. The victory of October confirmed the historically unprecedented foundations of the socialist way of life: the power of the workers in politics, public owner-

ship of the means of production in economics, and collectivism and comradely mutual assistance in human relations. In these revolutionary transformations is the inexhaustible source of the socialist system's vitality. All the international activity of the Communist Party of the Soviet Union is inspired with loyalty to the ideas of Lenin, whose principles of proletarian socialist internationalism and of peaceful coexistence are being fulfilled in the Soviet Union's foreign policy. The CPSU put forward the Peace Programme and is striving consistently for its implementation.

The Kremlin Palace of Congresses is a meeting place of the most important national gatherings. The 27th CPSU Congress was held here from February 25 to March 6, 1986.

Like a living heart, the Eternal Flame pulses at the Grave of the Unknown Soldier. The great Battle of Moscow in December 1941 ended in the first major defeat of the German fascist troops and heralded the collapse of Hitler's Reich. On 24 June 1945, a Victory Parade was held on Red Square. Scores of fascist banners and standards were hurled down at the base of the Mausoleum.

The unexampled heroism of the Soviet people will live forever, for they destroyed fascism in the greatest war known in the history of Mankind.

Forty years later...

On May 9, 1985 a parade to mark the 40th anniversary of the Soviet people's Victory in the Great Patriotic War was held in Moscow.

On that day war heroes paraded through Red Square. They were the people who had fought at the front, in partisan units and in the underground, who worked behind the lines, covered thousands of miles along wartime roads forty years ago and produced the weapons with which Victory was forged.

The legendary Victory banner flutters in the May breeze, the very banner that was hoisted over the captured Reichstag in the small hours of May 1, 1945.

May 9, the day we celebrate Victory, Peace and Development.

Thousands of red banners and posters... Music and songs...
Red Square is an unforgettable sight on festival days when
the working people of Moscow parade across it.

The administrative building of the Supreme Soviet of the USSR contains halls for sessions of the Soviet of the Union, the Soviet of Nationalities, and the Presidium of the Supreme Soviet.

These halls are used for the presentation of credentials by foreign ambassadors and for other diplomatic contacts between Soviet government representatives and foreign statesmen.

The building of the Council of Ministers of the USSR (formerly the Senate) is a remarkable example of Russian 18th-century architecture. This is the seat of the Soviet government, and it was here that Lenin lived and worked. The Sverdlov Hall, one of the finest round halls in the country, is situated in the east part of the building. It is unrivalled for originality of design and wealth of architectural forms. It is used on various ceremonial occasions.

Vladimir Ilyich Lenin lived and worked in the Kremlin, in the Soviet government building, from March 1918 to May 1923. Lenin's office was here. Next door to his office was the assembly hall of the Council of People's Commissars, the Council of Labour and Defence, and the Politburo of the Central Committee. From here Lenin directed the whole life of the country. Here, too, Lenin lived with his family in an apartment of four small and unpretentious rooms.

It is now a museum visited by people from all over the Soviet Union and abroad.

In the past, the Great Kremlin Palace was the temporary residence of the tsar's family while they were in Moscow. The palace is famous for its magnificent St George's Hall, so called in honour of the military order of St George the Victorious. In the deep niches and on the walls can be seen marble plaques bearing in gilt lettering the names of distinguished military units and Knights of St George. Amongst them are illustrious Russian military leaders and naval commanders.

St George's Hall is used for diplomatic and government receptions, the presentation of orders, and meetings between Party and government leaders and the working people.

The rooms on the ground and first floors of the Great Kremlin Palace are used for the reception of visitors from abroad.

The Terem Palace is a colourful building which houses what used to be the tsar's chambers. It was built by Russian architects Bazhen Ogurtsov, Antip Konstantinov, Trefil Sharutin and Larion Ushakov in 1635—1636. It is a magnificent monument of national architecture: the Russian craftsmen successfully captured in stone the character of folk wooden architecture.

The tsar's rooms consisted of the Anteroom, or passage, the Krestovaya Chamber, the Throne Room, or tsar's study, the Bedchamber and the Prayer Room. From the Throne Room, a narrow winding whitestone staircase leads to the Upper Little Terem and observation tower. There is something of an ancient fairytale about the multicoloured windowpanes, tiled stoves and painted walls.

Contemporaneous with the Terem Palace is the Upper Church of the Saviour, surmounted by eleven graceful gilded domes.

The Faceted Hall is Moscow's most ancient municipal building, put up in 1487—1491 by Russian craftsmen under architects Marco Fryazin and Pietro Antonio Solari for official ceremonies and solemn receptions.

The building was given its name from the faceted white-stone façade. The nine-metres-high rectangular hall impresses the visitor with a sense of space, light and festive majesty. The four vaults are supported by a single white-stone pillar in the centre.

It was here that Ivan the Terrible celebrated the fall of Kazan in 1552 and Peter the Great commemorated the victory at Poltava in 1709.

The Kremlin's Cathedral of the Annunciation. Its history goes back to 1397. At first, the cathedral had three domes and was not particularly large. In 1564, under Ivan the Terrible, it acquired nine domes. Work on it continued at various periods, but the artistic harmony and unity of style were preserved.

While the Cathedral of the Annunciation was being built, masons from Pskov raised the small, single-domed Church of the Deposition of the Robe (1484—1486). The style is very graceful, the murals being particularly noteworthy.

The Cathedral of the Assumption, the main building on Cathedral Square in the Moscow Kremlin, is simple and austere in style. Crowned by five cupolas, it is majestically beautiful. The walls are of hewn whitestone blocks, and the two rows of narrow windows are high above the ground level. The interior is magnificent.

The Kremlin ensemble is completed by the Ivan the Great Bell-Tower, a masterpiece of world architecture. Its history goes back to the times of Ivan Kalita. In 1600, the bell-tower was made higher and was surmounted with a gilded dome, after which its total height was 81 metres. Twenty-one bells cast by Russian master craftsmen of olden times have been preserved in the bell-cote and in the tower itself. At the foot of the Ivan the Great Bell-Tower stands the famous Tsar-Bell, 200 tons in weight. It was cast in 1733—1735 by Ivan and Mikhail Matorin.

The open-work grilles of the Cathedral of the Assumption
are marvellous examples of wrought iron. They impress
the visitor with their exquisite workmanship.

The paintings in the Cathedral of the Annunciation are truly amazing, and the icons by Theophanes the Greek, Andrei Rublev and Prokhor from Gorodets are priceless. The icons by Theophanes the Greek are both monumental and austere. Andrei Rublev's paintings have great warmth and sincerity, whereas there is much tension and drama in the icons by Prokhor from Gorodets.

The Cathedral of the Archangel boasts one of the most valuable of all ancient paintings, *The Archangel Michael* icon executed by Moscow artists at the end of the 14th and beginning of the 15th centuries. Many works of art dating back to the 11th—17th centuries are collected on the icon-ostasis of the Cathedral of the Assumption. Among them is the famous *St George* icon. The people's ideal of martial valour is symbolized by this courageous warrior.

The Kremlin Armoury is a unique treasure store of decorative and applied art. The museum's foundation dates back to the beginning of the 19th century. Of particular interest is the collection of ancient sidearms, firearms and military accoutrements: helmets, bows, quivers, arrows, sabres, swords, muskets, pistols, shields, coats of mail, and suits of armour. Some coats of mail consisted of sixty thousand fine rings weighing up to seventeen or, in the case of armour, up to ten kilogrammes. Altogether, over four thousand items of arms and armour are preserved in the building. The museum's oldest exhibit is the helmet of Prince Yaroslav, father of Alexander Nevsky (early 13th century).

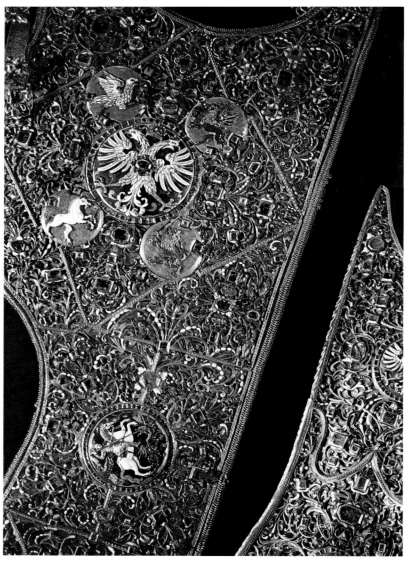

Carved gilt carriages, painted sleighs, shaft-bows, window frames, loving cups, salt-cellars, distaffs and benches—all these are genuine relics of folk art. Great talent and invention went into the fancy lace, open-work embroidery, and articles made by Russian armourers, stonecutters, metalworkers, jewellers, and niello craftsmen...

The Armoury is a repository for the most valuable objects in gold and silver, and in diamonds and other precious stones. Dippers, cups, vases, church plate, icon frames, table clocks and pocket watches—all impress the visitor with their beauty and originality. There is also a collection of fabrics and clothing.

The most ancient of the tsars' crowns preserved is the Cap of Monomakh, made by Oriental craftsmen in the 13th—14th centuries. The top of the crown is of the finest gold openwork welded on to a smooth sheet of gold. The Cap of Monomakh was used for the coronations of the Russian tsars.

Particularly rich in ornamentation are Tsar Mikhail Romanov's Great Regalia, made by craftsmen of the Moscow Kremlin in 1627—1628.

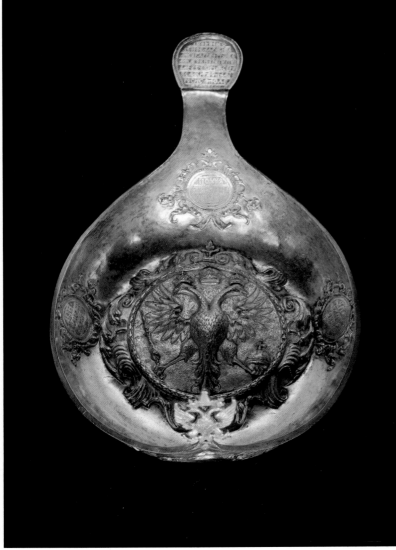

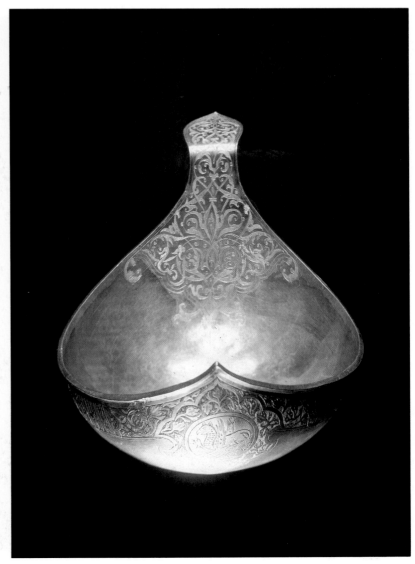

This memorial, created by sculptor Ivan Martos in 1804—
1815 and set up in Red Square in 1818, symbolizes the
majesty and indomitability of the Russian people. At the
beginning of the 17th century, Kuzma Minin and Dmitry
Pozharsky, in command of a volunteer army, drove the
Polish and Lithuanian interventionists out of Moscow.

In 1555—1561 a miracle of world art was built—the Cathedral of the Intercession (the Church of St Basil the Blessed),
commissioned by Ivan the Terrible to celebrate the final
deliverance of the Russian state from dependence on the
Kazan Khanate.
The domes of St Basil's, with their many different shapes
and colours, reflect the festive and joyful feelings inspired
by a great victory of the Russian people in ancient times.

64

The Kutafya Watch Tower stands opposite the Trinity Tower. In ancient times it was used to defend Trinity Bridge. In 1685, a superstructure was added to the Kutafya Tower, and it was decorated with an open-work parapet.

Many streets inside the Garden Ring have become protected zones. While new buildings are going up, ancient monuments are being restored, but the blend of different architectural styles is being carefully preserved. A master plan of reconstruction of the central part of the city to be completed in the year 2000 is now widely discussed by the public. Ancient monuments now provide a contrast to the contemporary building of the *Rossiya* Hotel. The little whitestone parish Church of the Conception of St Anne (late 15th—early 16th century) is one of the oldest stone churches outside the Kremlin.

The Bolshoi Theatre is the finest example of mid-19th-century Russian architecture. After the fire of 1853, the building (architects Osip Bove and Andrei Mikhailov) was reconstructed in 1855—1856 by architect Albert Kavos and sculptor Pyotr Klodt (the four horses on the pediment). In 1922, it was the venue for the First All-Union Congress of Soviets, which passed the resolution on the formation of the Union of Soviet Socialist Republics.

Architectural monuments of the 16th and 17th centuries have been restored on Razin Street: the English Courtyard, the Church of St Barbara, the Church of St Maxim the Blessed, and the buildings of the Old Royal Court.

A masterpiece of world architecture, "Pashkov's House" stands on the crest of a small hill opposite the Kremlin's Borovitsky Gates. The most beautiful house in Moscow, built in 1784—1786, it is the work of the great Russian architect Vasily Bazhenov (pages 74-75).

It was commissioned by Pashkov, a rich landowner. In 1862, it housed the State Municipal Library and the Rumyantsev Museum, and since 1925 it has been the premises of the Lenin State Library of the USSR.

Moscow's biggest railway termini, the Leningrad, Yaroslavl, and Kazan, are situated on Komsomolskaya Square. Lines run from here to the north, east and south of the Soviet Union.

The Kazan Terminus, built in 1912—1926, reflects all the decorative richness of ancient Russian architecture. The building reproduces the principle of the "khoromy", or mansion, style. After its reconstruction, now in progress, the Kazan Terminus will have facilities for seventeen thousand passengers which is four times as many as at present.

The tent-shaped roofs of the stone Yaroslavl Terminus building, the combination of light-coloured walls with dark roofs, and the patterned surfaces are reminiscent of the wooden architecture of the Russian North.

The Leningrad Terminus is famous. On 11 March 1918, a train arrived here from Petrograd with the Soviet government headed by Lenin.

In ancient times, the approaches to Moscow were guarded by monasteries which performed the function of defence works. In 1591 the guns of the Novodevichy Convent drove back the horde of the Crimean Khan Kazy-Girei when he tried to cross the Moskva River.

The centre of this ensemble is the Cathedral of the Virgin of Smolensk, built in 1524—1525 on the model of the Kremlin's Cathedral of the Assumption. It was here that Boris Godunov consented to become tsar of Russia. A graceful and decorative bell-tower dominates the convent. The buildings of the Lenin Central Stadium now stand on what were once the convent's water meadows in a bend of the Moskva River.

The viewing platform near Moscow University on Lenin Hills gives a magnificent panoramic view of the city: the arches of the bridges, the bends in the river, the stadium at Luzhniki, the Young Pioneer Palace, the Gorky Park...

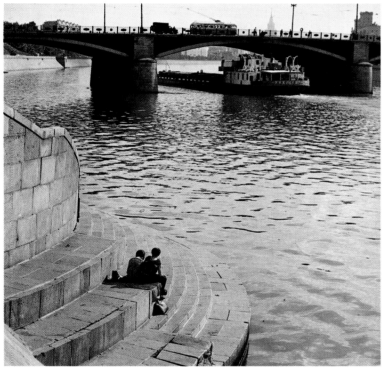

The Moskva River winds for hundreds of kilometres through the countryside round the capital, taking in many small streams on its way. The city receives grain, vegetables, metal, and timber through the river ports, and the products of Moscow's industries are sent to all the corners of the country. About five million passengers are carried annually by river boats on the city and suburban services.

There are over 60 embankments and over 300 bridges in Moscow. The Moskva River is the capital's precious blue girdle round the ancient hills of the city...

The buildings on Kalinin Prospekt and those of the Council for Mutual Economic Assistance and the Council of Ministers of the RSFSR have become symbols of contemporary Moscow.

In 1833—1836 the architect Yevgraf Tyurin supervised the construction of a new University building alongside the old one.

Once the palace of Moscow's governor-general, the building of the Moscow City Soviet of People's Deputies is the work of the famous architect Matvei Kazakov.

Gorky Street, one of Moscow's main thoroughfares.

Pushkinskaya Square.
The bronze monument to Alexander Pushkin, the great Russian poet, stands in the centre. Designed by sculptor Alexander Opekushin, it was put up in 1880. There are always fresh flowers at the foot of the memorial. The people's love for Pushkin is boundless.

Mayakovsky Square, one of the most important in the capital, is at the intersection of Gorky Street and the Garden Ring. In 1958 a monument was put up here, from a project by sculptor Alexander Kibalnikov, to the great Soviet poet Vladimir Mayakovsky.

In 1960 a 300-metre-long flyover crossed Krymskaya Square (part of the Garden Ring) to link Ostozhenka Street with Komsomolsky Avenue. On the right is what is known as Provision Warehouses, one of the finest monuments in the Russian Classical style, built in 1829—1831 to the design of Vasily Stasov.

Arbatskaya Square in Moscow.
The old Arbat Street together with side-streets is one of
the favourite districts of the Muscovites.
Many famous names in Russian culture are associated
with it.

Today Arbat is closed to traffic and has become a museum-street.

A memorial to the Patriotic War of 1812 has been erected on Kutuzovsky Avenue near Poklonnaya Hill. The heroic past of the Russian people comes to life again in Kutuzov's Hut and the Battle of Borodino Panorama museums. A unique work by Russian artist Franz Rubo, this enormous canvas, 115 metres long and 15 metres high, supplemented with lifelike models, recreates the authentic atmosphere of the famous battle.

Not far away stands another memorial to the Patriotic War of 1812 and a distinguished example of Russian architecture—the Triumphal Arch designed by Osip Bove. Victory Chariot surmounts the 28-metre-high arch.

The city's transport problem has been solved by the underground railway—that quickest and most comfortable form of travel. There are over 220 kilometres of track altogether on the Lenin Moscow Metro. Each day, its 138 stations take over seven million passengers. The best Soviet architects have worked, and are working, on the layout of the ground-level and underground halls. The Metro lines will eventually cater for the whole city.

Airlines connect Moscow with cities all over the Soviet Union. Aeroflot's comfortable high-speed aircraft regularly call at airports in 98 other countries. The Soviet air fleet carries over 100 million passengers every year.
A recent addition to Moscow's airports is Sheremetyevo-2, an international terminal with a hotel for transit passengers.

Moscow is a major junction of air, railway, water and road transport routes.

The freight turnover of the Moscow Railway is equal to that of all the railways in England, France and Italy taken together. Nearly one and a half million passengers pass through Moscow's nine railway termini every twenty-four hours.

Moscow University on Lenin Hills and the Lenin Central Stadium are linked by a two-tiered bridge, the lower part of which is a Metro station. It is the biggest bridge in Moscow: the river span is 198 metres and the upper tier over a kilometre long.

The architectural ensemble of the sports complex at Luzhniki is completed by the new Druzhba Multi-Purpose Sports Hall with space for 12 aspects of sport and comfortable stands for three to four thousand spectators. The unusual structure is reminiscent of a turtle shell.

Izmailovo, a major tourist centre, was erected in Moscow for the 1980 Olympics.

Of special interest is one of its main structures, an auditorium adorned with *A Paean to Man*, a monumental copper frieze by Zurab Tsereteli.

The opening ceremony of the 12th World Festival of Youth and Students took place in Moscow on July 27, 1985. The motto of the festival was "For Anti-Imperialist Solidarity, Peace and Friendship".

Over 20,000 delegates from more than 150 countries attended the Moscow forum.

The festival lasted for eight days. Its young participants, representing different nations, political views and religious beliefs, were unanimous in their eagerness to develop international contacts and exchange, to support peace, disarmament, freedom and justice and to maintain friendship and co-operation among nations. Their informal meetings and friendly discussions in Moscow helped the young people from different countries understand one another better and join their efforts for the sake of a better future for Earth.

Moscow, July 1986.
Some seventy countries of the world sent their best sportsmen to participate in the Goodwill Games. The noble spirit of these major international competitions is reflected in the very motto of the Games—"From Friendship in Sport—to Peace on Earth". Good will to peace, friendship, and the strengthening of understanding and trust among nations has united the strongest athletes of the planet who reiterated their loyalty to promoting the creation of a better and more secure world, the principles, proclaimed by the Olympic Charter.

The handsome semicircular building of the *Cosmos* Hotel stands across the street from the main entrance to the National Economic Achievements Exhibition of the USSR. It was designed jointly by Soviet and French architects. The new structure blends naturally with the exhibition park and pavilions (page 121).

Here, too, is Vera Mukhina's famous stainless steel sculpture, *The Worker and the Collective Farm Girl*. There is also the skyward-soaring titanium monument to the Conquerors of Space (page 120).

The flight on 12 April 1961 of the first manned spaceship was the greatest event of the 20th century and the beginning of a new era in the history of science. It was Yuri Gagarin, a citizen of the Soviet Union, who blazed the trail into space.

After the first solo flights came the team work. Soviet cosmonaut Alexei Leonov was the first to step out of a spaceship's hatch and demonstrate that man could live and work in open space. The Soviet Union regards space research as a vital task in the exploration and taming of the forces and laws of nature in the interests of the working people and for the sake of peace on Earth.

The Soviet Union comes out for far-reaching international co-operation in space for the good of man; it is resolutely working to stop the arms race, and acts with determination for a peaceful outer space, against the "star wars" policy.

Space techniques are increasingly being applied in the study of natural resources and in geographical and oceanological research.

Zvyozdny Gorodok (Star City), where the Soviet cosmonauts live and work, is not far from Moscow.

The world's highest reinforced concrete TV tower and the biggest TV centre in Europe are situated near the Ostankino Palace Museum (see pages 126-127).

The history of the Bolshoi Theatre of the USSR goes back to 1776. Its first actors, singers and dancers were gifted serfs or pupils from the orphanages. Since then, such magnificently talented artists have appeared on the theatre's opera stage as Fyodor Chaliapine, Leonid Sobinov, Antonina Nezhdanova, Nadezhda Obukhova, Valeriya Barsova, Alexander and Grigory Pirogov, Ivan Kozlovsky, Sergei Lemeshev, Mark Reizen, Pavel Lisitsian... In our days, too, the Bolshoi Theatre is famous for its wealth of vocal talent. The whole world knows the names of Irina Arkhipova, Yevgeny Nesterenko, Yelena Obraztsova, Vladimir Atlantov, Tamara Sinyavskaya, Zurab Sotkilava and other outstanding singers.

The traditions of the Moscow ballet school are handed down from generation to generation. Yekaterina Geltser was followed by Viktorina Kriger, Olga Lepeshinskaya and Marina Semyonova. Galina Ulanova, twice Hero of Socialist Labour, has been called "a miracle of our time". Today the stage of the Bolshoi is adorned by a galaxy of talented ballet-dancers: Maya Plisetskaya, Yekaterina Maximova, Natalia Bessmertnova, Lyudmila Semenyaka, Vladimir Vasilyev, Mikhail Lavrovsky, Yuri Vladimirov... For over twenty years the theatre's ballet company has been under the direction of the well-known choreographer Yuri Grigorovich.

The repertoire of the Bolshoi Theatre includes operas and ballets by Glinka, Dargomyzhsky, Borodin, Tchaikovsky, Mussorgsky, Rimsky-Korsakov, Rossini, Bizet, Verdi, Puccini, Prokofiev, Khachaturyan, and other famous Russian or foreign composers. The theatre company puts on special productions of operas, ballets and concerts for the stage of the Kremlin Palace of Congresses.

Musical and theatrical Moscow is a world of drama and opera theatres, orchestras and dance companies. Deservedly popular are the Symphony Orchestra of the USSR, the Osipov Russian Folk Orchestra, the Alexandrov Red Banner Song and Dance Company of the Soviet Army, the Folk Dance Company under the direction of Igor Moiseyev, and the Beryozka Dance Company.

Symphony orchestra concerts in the Conservatoire, Tchaikovsky Hall, House of Trade Unions or factory palaces of culture are invariably a success. The Tchaikovsky International Competition, a true festival of world musical culture, is held in Moscow every four years.

Moscow owns the greatest historical, literary and artistic treasures not only of national, but of world importance. They are represented in the museums covering the history of the revolution, the natural sciences, the history of art, literature, and the memorial museums.

The Tretyakov Gallery is a national treasure of Russian visual art. The best of various periods and schools can be seen here: works by Rublev and Dionysius, Ivanov, Bryullov, Fedotov, Venetsianov, Perov, Aivazovsky, Kramskoi, Vasnetsov, Vereshchagin, Vrubel, Savrasov, Levitan, Yaroshenko...

Valentin Serov. *Pond Overgrown With Weeds.*

Ilya Repin and Vasily Surikov have a special place in the history of Russian visual art. Their paintings represent the work of the *Peredvizhniki* (Travellers) at its finest. These artists not only developed the progressive democratic traditions of Russian painting but raised it to a new social level. They handled themes from the life of the ordinary people, celebrated the beauties of the Russian countryside, so full of poetic inspiration, revealed the spiritual wealth of man and appealed to his sense of civic responsibility. It was in the paintings by Repin and Surikov that Russian history was seen in all its true vitality for the first time. *The Zaporozhye Cossacks Writing a Letter to the Turkish Sultan,* a study for the famous picture by Repin, is full of penetrating wit and humour.

The Execution of the Streltsy by Vasily Surikov (detail), a vivid reflection of the complex and contradictory Petrine era.

The Tretyakov Gallery is famed for its works by Soviet painters of very different styles and creative vision. This collection gives a full idea of the lines of development followed by Soviet visual art: for instance, paintings by Petrov-Vodkin, *Interrogation of the Communists* by Ioganson, and *The New Moscow* by Pimenov.

The Pushkin Museum of Fine Arts is a repository of cultural treasures from the Ancient East, Rome, Greece, and Western Europe.

The museum's art gallery features works by the leading schools of art—Italian, Spanish, Dutch, Flemish and others. The art of painting is represented by Perugino, Botticelli, Boltraffio, Giulio Romano, Rembrandt, Rubens, Van Dyck, Murillo, Cranach... The museum owns one of the most extensive collections of French painting, including masterpieces by Nicolas Poussin, Jean Chardin, Louis David, Eugène Delacroix, Pierre Auguste Renoir, Edgar Degas, Paul Cézanne, Vincent van Gogh, Paul Gauguin, Henri Matisse and Pablo Picasso.

Perugino. *Madonna and Child.*

Rembrandt. *Portrait of an Old Woman.*

Many places in Moscow are associated with famous names in Russian literature and art.
The Tolstoy House Museum in Khamovniki. The authentic furniture (including the desk in Leo Tolstoy's study which he actually used in winters from 1882 to 1901 when he lived in the house) and the writer's personal belongings are carefully preserved here.
An old mansion on Kropotkinskaya Street is now the Pushkin Museum.

Masterpieces of Russian art created by the work and genius of serf craftsmen can be seen in the unique collections on the estates of Arkhangelskoye, Kuskovo and Ostankino.

The Ostankino Palace Museum of Serf Art happily combines this surviving example of old Russian architecture with landscaping that dates back to the end of the 18th century. The palace was built by talented Russian serf architects Mironov, Dikushin and Argunov. Although the palace is built of wood, it gives the impression of being a monumental stone structure. The interior is incomparable.

In the first quarter of the last century Prince Yusupov began rebuilding the estate of Arkhangelskoye, leaving the management of the work in the talented hands of serf architect Strizhakov. He was helped by Borunov, Ivan and Grigory Bredikhin, and Rabutovsky, also serf architects. The finishing work was done by serf craftsmen—cutters, gilders, metal-chasers and weavers. The museum displays original furniture, elegant candelabra and wonderful paintings. The collection of pictures includes works by Giovanni Battista Tiepolo, Hubert Robert, Charles Le Brun, Van Dyck, Bernardo Bellotto and other famous artists.

The park terraces, decorated with sculptural groups and statues, still lend beauty to this part of the Moscow countryside.

In Moscow there are many such residential areas near the river or a forest. It is quiet here, with plenty of greenery and clean, fresh air.

Remarkable monuments of ancient architecture can be seen in the Kolomenskoye Estate Museum, the old country residence of the Russian tsars and now inside the city limits.

The Church of St. John the Baptist (the church at Dyakovo) was put up during the reign of Ivan the Terrible in the mid-16th century. In 1532, the famous Church of the Ascension was built, the first stone tent-roofed structure of its kind in Russia, still impressive for its architectural originality and beauty.

Unique monuments of Russian wooden 17th-century architecture have been moved to the museum grounds, including the gate tower from the Nikolo-Korelsky Monastery (p. 157).

Rime-covered trees, a steep slope down to the river...
The miracle of spring, the time when nature awakens. We
wait for the warm days of summer too—the swimming, the
scent of hay, honey and apples... Autumn is beautiful in
its own way with its golden-purple patterns and the acrid
fragrance of mushrooms and of fallen, rain-sodden leaves.
But we have a very special love for the Russian winter.

The snow-covered Moscow boulevards look like a scene from a fairy-tale. It's difficult to imagine nature in Russia without winter.

This typical old Moscow private house on Kropotkinskaya Street is now a literary museum of Leo Tolstoy, the great writer of the Russian land.
The building was put up in 1817—1822 from a design by architect Afanasy Grigoryev.

"Moscow, a city to this day unknown to Europe, has six hundred or even eight hundred palaces, the beauty of which exceeds everything known to Paris," wrote Stendhal, who went to Russia in 1812 with the Napoleonic Army. Particularly rich in classical forms is this palace-type building which was put up in 1798-1802 by serf architect Kiselnikov and which is known as the Yauza Hospital. Particularly striking about this structure, which has been moved back from the street, is the majestic and richly decorated portico. The front courtyard is separated from the street by wrought-iron railings with elaborate gate pylons.

169

There are many unique architectural monuments in Moscow. On the corner of Armyansky Street and Bogdan Khmelnitsky Street, with a contemporary building as background, stands the Church of Sts Cosmo and Damian, built by Kazakov in 1791—1793. A special feature of the church is the almost total absence of decorative detail.

On Leningradsky Avenue the eye is caught by the Petrovsky Palace, also built by Kazakov in the late 18th century. It was here that the tsar could relax before riding into Moscow. The high stone wall and the corner towers suggest a fortress. Crowned with a dome, the two-storey brick palace stands at the back of the courtyard. The decorative details have been done in white limestone. The palace is now the Zhukovsky Air Force Academy.

Moscow is beautiful in all seasons.

The wind sweeps the snow dust off the domes of the Kremlin's ancient churches and spreads it over the streets and squares. In mid-winter, when the frosts array the trees in rime, even stone and metal seem benumbed with the cold.

"*Kremlin by winter moonlight over city and river,*" wrote the poet Alexander Tvardovsky, "*both Moscow named, With your Ivan the Great domed bell-tower and sombre guardian walls far-famed... Kremlin bathed in the winter moonlight, With many a thrilling ancient story, Your walls, domes, towers are illumined, As with your recent hard-won glory... On every corner, every bastion, There glow, with radiance unseen, Stalingrad, Leningrad, and proudly Our banner high above Berlin.*"

Centuries have passed over the sacred walls of the Kremlin. The stone fairy-tales and legends of Borovitsky Hill have become a source of inspiration to the creators of many architectural masterpieces.

Even when the temperature is thirty degrees centigrade below zero, there is a crowd near the Lenin Mausoleum on Red Square.

There are many places in Moscow associated with Lenin's name. One of the most recent memorial sites is Oktyabrskaya Square. On November 5, 1985, a monument to Lenin, a great thinker and revolutionary, the founder of the Communist Party of the Soviet Union and the world's first socialist state, was ceremonially unveiled there.
The monument was designed by sculptors Lev Kerbel and Vladimir Fyodorov and architects Gleb Makarevich and Andrei Samsonov.

Moscow carefully preserves the precious relics of the past.
The harmonious blend of ancient architectural monuments
with contemporary buildings gives the Soviet capital an
appearance that is entirely its own.
At night, the glow of the city lights can be seen from afar;
it is like the Milky Way that sends its light from outer space
to us on Earth below...